Robert Garnham has been performing comedy poetry around the UK for over twelve years at various fringes and festivals, theatres and poetry events. He has made a few short TV adverts for a certain bank, and a joke from one of his shows was listed among the funniest of the Edinburgh Fringe. He was recently an answer on the TV quiz show Pointless. Lately he has been writing short stories for magazines and a humorous newspaper column.

During his career he has performed on a moving train, in a florist's, on a boat and on a bus, as well as headlining at the legendary LGBT Duplex Cabaret in New York. He has won poetry slams in London, Edinburgh, Exeter and Totnes. He also provides vocals and lyrics for the experimental jazz fashion band Croydon Tourist Office.

His inspirations are eclectic and include Laurie Anderson, Ivor Cutler, Salena Godden, Rachel Pantechnicon, Douglas Adams, Pet Shop Boys, John Hegley, Alan Bennett, Jerry Seinfeld, Pam Ayres, Dandy Darkly, Frank O'Hara, MargOH! Channing, David Byrne and Spalding Gray.

www.professorofwhimsy.com

CU01509736

Yay!

Robert Garnham

Burning Eye

BurningEyeBooks
Never Knowingly
Mainstream

This edition published by Burning Eye Books 2021

www.burningeye.co.uk

@burningeyebooks

Burning Eye Books
15 West Hill, Portishead, BS20 6LG

ISBN 978-1-913958-02-2

Yay!

To Jill and David

CONTENTS

SEASIDE SERENADE

It must be hot.
My Mars bar's turned to mush,
The smell of melting tarmac
In the late-night hush.
Bread in the packet has already turned to toast.
My neighbour's pet chicken is now a Sunday roast.
Now, I don't like to boast,
But I've got Brandon, ooooh, Brandon
Basking on my bed in his boxers,
Both of us pining for something fresh,
Other than the obvious.
Like the steering freeze of truth,
The cool, cool wash of contentment,
Or a vanilla ice cream.

We're making our way through this
Seaside town now, me and Brandon.
He's promised something hot and long and sticky
The moment we get back.
It's been years since I had a kebab.
Past shop clad shutters and graffiti denouncing
Tracey as a slag
To the neon buzz moth hub
Of the prom prom prom,
Tiddly om pom pom.
Last night in bed he said,
'It isn't very long,
Tiddly om pom pom,
And it's very limp.'

And I said,
'It's seen a lot of tourists over the years,
And it's prone to erosion
And longshore drift.
Half of it was swept away
By a giant squid.'

The rash on the side of my neck
Is caused by Brandon's stubble as it scrapes,
Sandpaper scrapey sprapey scrape,
When he gets distracted by
The cricket results.

And now we're walking next to the beach and his face is
Lit up like that of a cartoon ferret on a box of cheap own-brand
Rice Krispie knock-offs,
The spoon filled with ricey goodness
Hovering inches from his cavernous gob.

And the salt air late-night sea breeze
Caresses our manly frames,
Instilling in us all kinds of nautical hijinks,
Naval seriousness, merry little frigates,
Dolphin blowholes, bottom-feeding mullets,
Whales both humpback and sperm,
First mate officers, salty sea dogs,
Able-bodied seamen, bow thrusters,
Butt blocks in the rigging, man the head,
Bump head gurnards and bottle-nosed lumpsuckers.
And chub.

Do you see the ice cream van?
Do you see the ice cream van?
An oblong of light spilled out on the
Sand-flecked concrete,
Its refrigeration generator
Throbbing the sir with a sudden intensity,
Chugga chugga chugga.
Do you feel it throbbing away there?
Chugga chugga chugga.
Window stickers advertising all kinds
Of things to lick and nibble and crunch down on,
Cool and ever so creamy.

The moon beams on high like someone from Dorset.
In the glow of its madness we dance.

Oh, Brandon, I want to do things
To certain bits of you
For most of the night,
Though I'm conscious you've got an early shift
At the Lady Remington Smooth 'n' Silky
Cordless Rechargeable Hair Removal Facility factory.
And the ice cream man,
Oh,
The ice cream man,
Did I mention he's also a magician?
A sparkle in his eye,
He starts waving his magic wand at us, and

Poof!

All is gone.
The ice cream man is gone.
The ice cream van is gone.
The neon and the stats are gone.
And Brandon is gone.
None of them ever existed.
It's just me, and the prom
On a sultry night in a sleepy coastal town,
And the kebab shop is closed,
And the rash on my neck
Is just a fungal infection,
And Tracey is still a slag, apparently,
And I walk sadly home.
I walk sadly home.

SEASIDE SOUL

This town is not torrid, nor tainted nor brazen,
This tornado of flavours,
Chip shops and chopsticks and packets of Quavers.
Savour its layers and nautical sailors.

Barbers and harbours and car parks and Mars bars,
A beer at the Pier Inn while peering at the pier thing,
A stride and a stroll,
But hide from the gulls your hot sausage rolls.
It's the way that we roll
With our seaside soul.

High-tide drip-dry knick-knack paddywhack,
Picnic and a pack-a-mac,
Promenade flapjack,
Sand in your rucksack,
Sand in your flapjack,
Sand in your arse crack.
Let's go to the pub.

Cinema chick flicks,
Candyfloss, pick 'n' mix,
Fish 'n' chips, kiss me quick,
Think I feel sick!

Ring road surf shack seaweed stink.
Caravan holiday:
It's worse than you think.
Dodgy dodgy plumbing and a blocked-up sink.
Big bands and jazz hands, gleaming sands and
One-night stands.
You probably will not understand.
It ain't no hole
With your seaside soul.

Amusements, bemusement,
Soup of the day,

The all-day breakfast
Only served till midday.
Have you paid and displayed?
Grab your bucket and spade!
You'll never be dismayed.
Memories fade,
But your heart will always stay.

This frisky town, this sea breezy town,
This cream tea scene of green seas and freezing dips,
Donkey rides and cheesy chips,
Ice cream by the bowl:
We've got seaside soul.

Dancing like lovers on the prom in the rain,
The hot pulse of life adding fire to my brain,
The legs of the pier stride deep in the brine.
Let's dance once more time, say you'll be mine.
We laugh and we grin and we howl at the ships.
The night is afire and it smells just like chips
You bend for a kiss like a child with a doll.
You ask what's for dinner; I say seaside soul.

TOM

Chisel-chinned trendy wordsmith,
All teeth and tan and hair
That looks like it could be easily quiffable,
So young and clean he's probably easily sniffable,
Thou hipster Ginsberg with a
Conscience so hot it can
Warm the coldest day with the
Fires of righteousness,
Whose words ooze sensibility.
How pained his outlook, this
Zeitgeist-bending Twitter-trending
Hot young thing, this
New kid on the writer's block, this
Prototype Byron with exuberant facial expressions,
This slam-winning rhyme-spinning nonchalant
Thin thin slip of a lad with a gob that spews
Perfect indignation in just the right amounts
With controlled anger
And lots of dramatic
.
.
.
.
.
.
.

Pauses.

Oh God, I wish he were me.

I wish I could be him. I wish he and I
Were mutually interchangeable.
He's so brilliant, like the brightest object
In the known galaxy, a supernova,
A thousand fires of phosphorous force,

Brilliant at what he does,
Brilliant at capturing souls,
Brilliant at poetry.
I bet he's brilliant at everything.
I bet he's never lost a game of Buckaroo.

He's brilliant and sexy and worthy and oh so right
And sexy and coolly infused into the very now
And sexy and young with the most perfect skin
That he should merely stand at the mic and open
His mouth and utter two syllables for me to become as flustered
As a Victorian gentleman who's just
Caught his first glimpse of ankle.

And I want to speak to him,
I want to commune with him,
I want to tell him, *Good stuff, man.*
You've opened my mind to new possibilities
And then trampled on it with your youthfulness,
In your trendy Converse All Stars with no socks,
As you lift the night completely to the very pinnacle
Of absolute truth
And by turns remind me that my own youthfulness
Is now as relevant and erroneous
As turning up at an otter convention
With a stoat.

Oh, this slippy hippy snake-like lad,
All very subtle and very emotey.
If you didn't know any better
You'd think him a bit scrotey,
So slight and wild in the night,
Afire with the rhythms of poets past.
I want to speak to him,
Whisper so subtly into his ear,
Blow me,
Blow me away with your words.
I love your body,
I love your body,

I love your body
Of work.

And at the break, people are talking,
Eulogising, rhapsodising,
And it's all about him, oh,
For he's so intense and righteous and theatrical
And oh,
He's so vibrant and ravishing and clever
And oh,
He's so visionary and brash and emotional
And oh,
Not only that, but he's got the kind of forearms
That could easily operate a butter churn with
Hardly any trouble at all
(This gig being in an arts centre in Dorset,
Where butter churns are obviously still a thing).

I follow him
Through this crowd of admirers and acolytes,
Tiptoeing on the periphery
Of a youthful mini mob,
Suddenly aware that I'm the only one there
Who remembers the millennium,
Or Tamagotchis,
Or the 1984 Olympics.

He makes a break for the bogs,
And now we're at neighbouring urinals,
The fluorescent tubes of this magical wazza
Gently caressing the soft hairs of his delicate chin,
His eyes scanning the blank tiled wall,
His sensitive nostrils
Taking in the pungent earthy aromas
In a venue where the patrons are mostly
Vegetarian and as such
Relish the most intriguing bowel movements.

His eyes almost feral and yet

With deep intelligence
As he concentrates on the matter at hand
With the same kind of intensity
He demonstrates at the mic,
His pee stream strong,
And healthy, and forceful.
It sounds like the Trevi Fountain;
It's certainly just as aesthetically pleasing.
He doesn't even fart.
Is there anything
He's not good at?

And I want to tell him
That I loved his poems.
All of his poems.
His poem about oxygen
Was such a breath of fresh air;
His poem about raspberries
Was surprisingly bitter;
His poem about the Mona Lisa
Was a masterpiece;
His poem about the perfect serve in tennis,
I couldn't fault it;
His poem about being woken by the smoke alarm,
Such an eye-opener,
And I want to tell him
That I got the joke he put in
About déjà vu,
Even though I'd heard it before.

And I want to tell him
That he's changed the way I look at the world,
And I want to tell him
That he speaks with a clarity of conscience so concise
He makes the Dalai Lama look like a mardy
Self-centred Premiership footballer,
And I want to tell him
That his voice is so silky smooth,
Listening to him is just like

Nuzzling a mallard,
And I want to tell him
That I'd pay him thirty quid and a packet of Frazzles
For just a very brief snog,
And I want to tell him
That his skinny jeans really
Leave nothing to the imagination.

And I want to tell him
That his work evokes such feelings within,
Destiny and timelessness,
The sheer manic dance of life,
Magic in the mundane,
A pounding euphoric oneness
That weaves us all into that
Inescapable yet brilliant tapestry of life.
This is what I want to tell him,
But instead I stare at his knob.

We wash our hands at the sink,
And as I wait for the hand dryer,
Which has all the power of
A gnat's fart,
I say,

'Hey, good set,'
And he says,
'Cheers.'

A YAK IN THE BACK OF THE CAR

You gave me a lift home,
But you had a yak in the back of the car.
I wanted to tell you how much I loved you,
But you had a yak in the back of the car.
I said, 'Pull over to the hard shoulder;
I've got yak slobber
On my shoulder.'
It's hard to whisper sweet nothings
With yak slobber on my shoulder,
And you had a yak in the back of the car.

I'd planned all day to reveal my love
And make plans for our life together,
But when you pulled into the station forecourt
You had a yak in the back of the car.
My hopes and dreams lay as tattered
As the rancid fur on the flanks of the yak.
The yak in the back of your car.

We went to the McDonald's drive-through;
We both had Chicken McNuggets and the yak had a Big Mac.
In the long silence that followed as you drove
I slurped Pepsi Max and the yak kept farting.
The evening was not as romantic as I'd hoped.

I'd built up the night as being the one,
But the only intimacy I got was
The yak resting its big chin on the top of my head,
Its stubbly beard and its pungent aroma
Somehow reminding me of my Aunt Mavis.

At the traffic lights
Some youths pulled up next to us and yelled,
'Hey,
That thing belongs in a zoo!'
And the yak shouted back,
'He's the only one who can drive!'

You got out the car to pay
At the service station.
I tried to make small talk
With the yak.
I couldn't get anything out of it.
For an animal called a yak
It didn't talk very much,
And just as I was telling it how much
I loved you,
It threw up on my lap.

We snuck into a late-night bar,
You and me and the yak in a wig,
But it got mistaken for Boris Johnson
And we had to get the hell out of there.

As we drove we sang along
To late-night jazz,
You and me and the yak in the back.
Soulfully, its beautiful crooning
Fogged up the windows with yak breath.

And I wanted to say,
Hey, forget the yak,
I've got something to tell you:
I love you, and I always have.
But I couldn't, what with
The yak in the back of your car,
Who, incidentally,
Was the only one there who was
Even slightly horny.

A psychoanalyst might say,
We all have yaks,
Yaks in the backs of our cars,
To which I might respond,
Hey, I'm paying sixty quid an hour
For this bollocks.

And then, all of a sudden, you whispered,
'Hey, let's find a hotel and make out,'
And I replied,
'What about the *you-know-what*?'
And you said,
'It's an aphrodisi-yak.'

THE LAD ON THE BUS WATCHING PORN ON HIS PHONE

A midnight bus to oblivion,
More commonly known as Torquay.
A night out with friends ended
Prematurely, with the eternal ennui
Of farewells, and jocularity,
A last-minute wee
And an hour's bus ride back
To a late-night cup of tea.
I live life on the edge!

An apparition, a diesel throbbing angel,
It merges from the fog,
Number and bus route lit up
Like the scoreboard on Family Fortunes.
The driver could not be any less festive,
Waves me rearward with a cursory glance
At my ticket,
Pulls away sharply as I negotiate the stairs
And a puddle of congealed vomit
Which has rolled down the upstairs aisle
And resembles, bizarrely, the face of Stephen Fry.
And now it's dry,
Just like his humour.

I sit back in my seat
And let out a moan,
And that's when I realise
That I'm not alone.
There's a lad at the front,
And he's watching porn on his phone.

He's not heard me come up,
So engrossed is he in the erotic delights
On his tiny flickering screen,
His face a mask of deep concentration.
He looks like a constipated weasel

Who's just been told that the photocopier
Has jammed again.
He rocks from side to side, swayed by bus buffeting,
His shoulders slump as his signal stops buffering,
And me, I'm suffering,
Feeling awkward, trying not to look.

His phone screen lights his little corner,
The adjacent windows reflecting, on two sides,
Lots of limbs and flesh, and to be honest
I really can't tell what's happening and I'm
Trying to distract myself by memorising a
Pam Ayres poem.

He's wearing a hoodie with the hood up and a
Baseball cap and a thick coat and trackie bottoms,
And the poor lad must be hot under all those layers,
Unlike the man and the woman on his phone, who
Aren't really wearing much at all, though even I
Can tell that she's faking it,
And the man for some reason is wearing a
Deliveroo cyclist's uniform and one of those big boxes.
Straight people are weird.

The bus seat headrests form a valley of
Stagecoach orange plastic, at the end of which
His quivering mobile, held in landscape mode,
Acts like a cinema screen at a drive-in.
I ask myself, *What would Pam Ayres do?*
She'd wonder what kind of plan he was on.
Some of these videos use up a lot of mobile data.

So I've heard.

I try not to make a sound.
The 5p carrier bag from Poundstretcher is going
To get me in all sorts of trouble.
I kind of shift down in my seat a little bit.
Part of me is jealous, not only for the brazenness of youth,

The readily available content and
His healthy spirit of sexual experimentation,
But also because he managed to grab
The seat right at the very front.

A dual carriageway, the bus engine
Whines and throbs and roars,
Picks up speed.
This sudden velocity
Only feeds his impetuosity.
He turns up the sound; the rhythmic groaning,
The sighing and the sultry sax combine
With a crunch of gears and brakes and exhaust
And the ceaseless squelch of rubber tyres
On wet tarmac as this thrusting double decker
Noses its way down through the hinterlands
Like an inquisitive haberdasher,
Chugging and shuddering and swaying and rocking,
And over the noise and the roar and the wind rush
I just about make out the words
From his tinny speaker,
'Hello, my name is Troy, where would you like the pepperoni?'

Hoodie Boy lowers his hood.
He's got a tattoo behind his ear in Chinese script,
Which I momentarily mistake for the Lidl corporate logo.
The bus slows for a stop in a nowhere town.
He puts down his phone and cups his hands against the window,
Sighs deeply, as if suddenly conscious of
All the pain in the world, ennui, inconsequentialities,
The finite nature of human existence, environmental disaster,
The meaningless of life itself, and all the wrongs
Of society.
Seeing my reflection, he jumps, then says,
'It's foggy out there, isn't it?'
To which I reply,
'I don't know,
I wasn't watching!'

INSTRUCTIONS FOR MY FUNERAL

My friend Anne has planned her funeral.
She wants bright colours,
All the colours of the rainbow,
Beach wear and party glitter,
Pink feather boas and dancing,
Cocktails and music and laughter,
Because, she says, 'Life is a chase,
A dream; why not celebrate,
Obscure the hate,
Spread joy in the moment before it's too late
To expose the beauty that lies deep within
Every pristine soul?'
Have you ever heard such bollocks?

I want sobbing at my funeral.
Uncontrollable sobbing.
Mourners dressed in black, sobbing,
In an austere church with such bad acoustics
That all you can hear is sobbing.
I want horses with those black tassels on their heads,
And I want the horses to look sad,
And if possible I want the horses to be sobbing, too.
I want dreary music, and just when it sounds
Like the dreary music is about to end,
I want it to start up again.
Dreary music and sobbing.

I want a sermon which goes on and on
And is so incredibly pointless
That not even the vicar knows what it's about.
I want the vicar to be a droner.
A droner with a nasal whine,
Bad teeth and dandruff.
I want the vicar to talk about how
Meaningless life is.
I want the pews to be
Really uncomfortable.

I want my casket to be there, of course.
I want someone to throw themselves on it
And have to be dragged away.
I want some poor sucker to have to
Read some poem by a Brontë sister.
I want my gravestone to read,
Sleep brings no joy to me.
And I want the stock markets to crash
That very morning
Just because of my death.
And I want it to rain.
You know the sort of rain.
That wet rain.
And I want the pallbearers
All to get a slipped disc.
And on the way home
The mourners stop at a café
And order chips,
But the waitress says
That the fryer has broken,
So they order jacket potatoes instead,
But the jacket potatoes are still raw in the middle
And the salad is limp.

I want my death to come
At a period of maximum inconvenience
For everyone,
Right at a time of peak happiness
Or just before a long-anticipated holiday.
I want people to have to cancel things.
I'm laughing about it right now.
I want my death to be so, so miserable
That it reminds people of Worcestershire.
Oh my God,
That's what I want.

Anne says she wants to put the fun
Back into funeral,

And she's already bought a CD of S Club 7
Just in the off-chance.
But I, oh, I
Aspire to greater things.
In fact, it's a shame
I won't be around to see it.

I'M IN LOVE WITH A MAGICIAN

You sawed me in half and I loved it.
Just a stage trick, of course; you
Amazed people with your two rings and
That was always your big opening, a flash,
A puff of smoke and a flock of doves which
The theatre manager had to have exterminated
After they defecated
On his organ.

I'd twiddle your moustache and we'd
Saunter through strange city streets, your
Flailing cape wrapping round my legs, and
When a group of street thugs
Pulled a knife you took off your top hat
And pulled out a rabbit,
And they said, 'Ahh, cute,
Look at its little whiskers.'

In the next town, in neon above the theatre,
The Great Splendido Is Magic All Over the World!
Though you were not magic
In the one place where it counted,
And your name was actually John.
We passed a fashion outlet.
'Fat Face,' you said.
'No need to be so cruel,' I replied.
'And, by the way, I haven't seen your magic wand
For a few weeks now.'

You were never an intellectual.
Your email log-in was Abracadabra.
Your magic didn't pay the rent.
'Eat some bread,' you said.
'It won't fill me up,' I replied,
'Even though it says wholemeal on the packet.'

'I can't just conjure love out of thin air,'

You said.
That night on stage at the
Nuneaton Vegetable Growers Club
A woman threw a swede at you.
His name was Sven.
And the greatest trick you ever pulled
Was that I became invisible.

Then followed the longest of nights.
Just like your pocket handkerchief,
It went on and on,
And I'd think of the times we'd spent angrily
Practising catching bullets between our teeth,
Shooting our mouths off,
And I'd say, 'Oh, this is so infuriating.
You make me want to pull my hair out!'
And you'd reply, 'I use a rabbit,
Ha ha ha ha ha,
I use a rabbit.'

Those times I thought my heart was beating
It was just Mr Nibbles curled up in your hat.

In the morning I woke; you'd disappeared.
I drank my tea from the mug you'd never used,
Being a sorcerer.
I gazed out the window at the overcast sky
And I knew I'd soon forget you,
And how you'd arrive for your act
In a blinding flash and some smoke,
Rising up by means of a trapdoor.

And me?
I was that trapdoor,
Or that's how it felt.
I was just a stage
You were going through.

I'M IN LOVE WITH A CLOWN

There's a man I love. I might have issues,
But I fancy him; he's got such big shoes.
You know what that means.
It doesn't need explaining.
Let me tell you, ladies, I'm
Certainly not complaining!

I heard him once saying that he
Liked to ride on Michael.
I didn't realise this was his
Unicycle.
He's so macho,
He's so randy,
He's got a giant hooter; well,
That'll come in handy.

We made out on the sofa
Most evenings.
When he wore stilts he got
Cobwebs off the ceiling.
He won't tease me,
He won't hurt me,
He let me sniff his plastic flower
And never once did squirt me.

Twenty of his friends one day,
They all came over.
All of them were crammed into
A Nissan Micra.
He'll be with me
Until the day I die.
I almost lost my nose in his
Light-up spinning bowtie.

When we kiss I get
Make-up on my chin
And in other places; it

Depends where I've just been.
He chucks custard pies
In people's faces.
He always gets unnecessary
When I snap his braces.

We spent so many nights
In an erotic dance.
I would get turned on
By his baggy pants.
He would repeat my name
Like some kind of worship.
I tried to do the same to him,
But his name was Parsnip.

But he left me once,
One lonely frosty morning.
He didn't leave a note and
There was no warning.
A quiet squeaking
Slowly receding.

My heart was bleeding.
Cobwebs on the ceiling.

He didn't want to hurt me.

I suppose it was a nice
Jester.

THE CIRCUS OF MEDIOCRITY

Roll up!
Roll up!
Everyone!
Under the big top tonight,
The most average things in
The entire universe!
The Circus of Mediocrity!

We've got a peep show,
A freak show,
We've got everything you'd seek, though,
At just under fifteen quid,
It's not exactly a cheap show!
It's touring everywhere
From Basingstoke to Chepstow.
Wheelchair access is poor
Because of all the steps, though.
It's the Circus of Mediocrity!

The big top isn't very big;
The whole thing shrank in the rain.
The clowns all look the same.
The acrobats
Are matter-of-fact,
And the tightrope walker never came
The tumblers are all head over heels;
It really is a shame.
We haven't got a lion
For the lion tamer to tame,
But we have got a badger
With a chip on its shoulder.
It's the Circus of Mediocrity!

It's a beautiful tradition,
But please, with our permission,
Have a look at the condition
Of the rusted-up trapeze.

It all was once admired,
But now it's all quite tired,
And the human cannonball was fired.
The whole thing's on its knees.
It's the Circus of Mediocrity!

It's hard to drum up fun
When you're feeling pretty glum
And, for the fifth time today,
The acrobat has landed on his bum.
The audience in Okehampton
Numbered twenty-one,
And one of those was my mum.
Please, oh, please do come
To the Circus of Mediocrity!

We raise the big top
But not your hopes.
It's more than just the tightrope walker
Who's on the ropes.
Our comedian is glum;
You should see how he mopes.
Our profits are so tiny
You need microscopes.
Oh, the alarm, the anxiety!
It's such a nonentity!
It's the Circus of Mediocrity!

Every night our manager
Has a big strop
Under the big top.
He's got a big flop.
It's called the Circus of Mediocrity!

The knife thrower couldn't give a toss.
The whole thing's run at a loss.
No one will admit to being the boss,
And the only people who are death-defying
Are those eating the candyfloss.

It's worse than you ever feared.
It really is so weird.
The magician has disappeared,
And the mind reader says he knows
Exactly what the audience is thinking.
The whole thing is stinking.
My hopes are sinking;
I've taken up drinking.
It's such an atrocity.
It's the Circus of Mediocrity!
It's the Circus of Mediocrity!

CUBICLE

Lusty gazes across the vestibule.
This sudden connection.
Adrenaline and sexualised emotions
Fed by diesel exhaust, locomotive momentum,
Two strangers intercontinental
Pushing open the zig-zag door of
The toilet cubicle.

You're cute.
No, you're cute.
Let's do this.

I pull the door closed.
It snags on my shoe.
Pull again a little too hard.
My hand slips and I
Accidentally punch him in the throat.
How handsome he looks as he
Bends over in agony
And in so doing headbutts me in
The chin.

Door closed.
Ocupado.

His face so tender
It enthrals the night, the throbbing
Engines whining in all their inter-city delirium.
Passion fills the cubicle as I
Help him remove his T-shirt,
My elbow scraping against the
Paper towel dispenser.
Ever so slyly he slips my T-shirt
Over my shoulders,
Steadying himself against the flush mechanism.
The toilet swallows my belt.
I take off my jeans and

Once again punch him in the throat.

'You feral rampant man,' he says.
'Just the smell of a train
Gets me all excited.'
'Hey,' I say,
'I did this once on an aircraft
While writing
Short Japanese poems.
I became a member of the
Mile haiku club.'
He doesn't laugh.

Passionately, we kiss.
My elbow activates the
Hand dryer.
'So hot,' he says, 'so hot.'
'Oh yes,' I reply.
'No, really,' he says, 'turn that thing off.'
He puts his arm around me and
Scrapes his knuckles on the
Plastic ceiling.
'Jesus Christ!' he yells.
I activate the flush button again.
He accidentally squirts
Hand soap all over the place.
The hand dryer comes on again.
Yet another flush.
I bang my head against the bulkhead.
He bangs his knees on the wall.
The tap comes on, then goes off,
Goes on, goes off.
Slippery and suddy on the hand soap floor,
I put my arm out to steady myself
And the toilet roll unwinds.

It's all so
Devastatingly romantic.

Then the train starts running over
Points and tracks and it all becomes bumpy.
We osculate amid the oscillations,
Steadying ourselves as the train
Rocks from side to side
Like a salad of passion in a bowl
Of steamy lust
Drizzled with the
Vinaigrette
Of regret.
'Am I the only one,' I say,
'Who gets turned on by
Self-service ticket machines?'
'Yes,' he says.
More bumping around.
Shook up with soapy suds and clumps of wet bog roll,
Flush, hand dryer, tap on and off,
One hand briefly trapped in the
Sanitary towel bin.
'Oh my God,' he says,
'The ten fifteen service to Orgasm
Is ready to depart!'

Oh my.
We relax, lean back
Against the cubicle wall.
'Well,' he says,
'I think most of it went on the floor,
But that wasn't too bad.'

COCKY

Darren Cockburn was a grinning marionette.
Darren Cockburn was living in a maisonette.
Darren Cockburn was the first lad I met
At secondary school.
Darren Cockburn was a spiky-haired loon.
Darren Cockburn was a teenage buffoon.
Darren Cockburn was the lad I would soon
Pine for every day.
Darren Cockburn didn't know I was gay.
Nor did I.

Darren Cockburn was a demon resplendent in football kit.
Darren Cockburn was a cheeky git.
Darren Cockburn would probably have had a fit
If he knew how I felt.
Darren Cockburn was an aura of male hormones.
Darren Cockburn was all skin and bones.
Darren Cockburn went round his friends' homes
For dinner after school.
Darren Cockburn never came round mine.
I wanted him to come round mine.

Darren Cockburn was a raven-beaked sprite.
Darren Cockburn was not academically bright.
Darren Cockburn once set alight
A microwave during home economics.
Darren Cockburn got his finger caught in an art room easel.
Darren Cockburn's aftershave of choice was Diesel.
Darren Cockburn looked a bit like a weasel,
And since then I've always loved furry creatures.
Darren Cockburn was always in trouble with the teachers.

Darren Cockburn would smile at me at odd occasions.
Darren Cockburn distracted me from long equations.
Darren Cockburn would never be the voice of our generation,
Unless the only thing our generation had to say was a
Well-timed fart during assembly.

Darren Cockburn had skin so smooth like Devonshire cream.
Darren Cockburn was once my partner on the parallel trampoline.
Darren Cockburn had the best earlobes I'd ever seen,
And I'd seen a lot of earlobes.
Darren Cockburn, I liked him loads.

Darren Cockburn had a bright red polyester coat.
Darren Cockburn apparently owned a pet goat.
Darren Cockburn was probably a bit of a scrote,
But he was my scrote, all mine.
Darren Cockburn's dad once met Terence Trent D'Arby.
Darren Cockburn could be Ken to my Barbie.
Darren Cockburn tried to chat to me about the North London derby.
I have no idea what he meant.
I still don't now.
I don't know anything about horse racing.
Darren Cockburn got my heart racing.

Darren Cockburn, oh, I'd tell people he was my friend.
Darren Cockburn's nose was slightly upturned at the end.
Darren Cockburn once started a new trend
For carrying a tin of mackerel fillets in your shirt pocket.
Darren Cockburn was my absolute fave.
Darren Cockburn's dad installed cheap polystyrene architrave.
Darren Cockburn said he once went to a rave
But they wouldn't let him in.
Darren Cockburn is who I think about
When I see a mackerel fillet tin.

Darren Cockburn was beauty ensconced in a masculine frame.
Darren Cockburn, oh, how I shiver at the mention of his name.
Darren Cockburn, my God, it's such a shame
What the years have done.
Darren Cockburn disappeared after school: probably for the best.
Darren Cockburn sent me a Facebook friend request
Darren Cockburn, oh, how since school you have been blessed
With three kids and a bald head and a big big belly.
Darren Cockburn, my legs turned to jelly
When I saw your name on my screen.

Darren Cockburn, I let out a scream.
And then pressed
Ignore.
Because that's
What the past
Is for.

JESUS OF WOKING

Oh come, all ye faithful,
To the town square of a
Surrey suburb one pre-Easter Friday,
Whereat an avant-garde modern
Interpretation of the Crucifixion
Doth suddenly appear among
Primark shoppers, traffic wardens, and me.
A scaffolding pole cross,
Soldiers in army fatigues, and Jesus himself,
In black football shorts and
Nothing else,
And lo,
For he is buff.

He's a beefcake Jesus in a
Builder's hard hat,
A male model son of God
Shackled to S and M scaffolding
Outside M and S,
And I've
Quite forgotten what it was
I needed in Lidl.

A banner reads,
Woking United Churches are
Excited to stage their own
Interpretation of the Crucifixion.
And I'm excited
For entirely different reasons.

He's been roughed up, duffed up,
And for some strange reason
He's been oiled up,
Now hung up on the makeshift cross
In a manner spookily reminiscent
Of *Fifty Shades of Grey*
Chapters six, eight, eleven, fifteen,

Twenty-three, twenty-eight, thirty-one,
Thirty-five,
And also from some of my old VHS videos.

And it's Friday, and it's drizzling,
And there's a poster advertising cheap cat litter,
And a young man a similar age to me
(Early twenties)
Is shackled to scaffolding
In skimpy Adidas football shorts
Which really leave nothing to the imagination,
And he's
Writhing and groaning with ecstasy,
And Edith Hepplewhite from number twenty-six
Has just walked into a lamppost,
And how I would like to fall to my knees
In absolute devotion
Even though the tattoo on his shoulder blade reads
I Loves Ya Becky.
Oh, he's a macho and masculine messiah,
A Chippendale Christ,
Erect and proud for all to see.
Oh, oh, oh, Jesus Christ!

The procession carrying his cross
Goes through some low overhanging branches,
Then stops just short
Of the railway bridge.
I sit down and
Eat a scotch egg.

YOU DUNKED A MUFFIN IN YOUR CUPPA

I thought you were a real fun guy.
We got on well, didn't have to try.
But what you did just made me cry.
You dunked a muffin in your cuppa.

I know that you're a sexy hunk,
But I was almost sick when I saw you dunk.
Your muffin is now a sodden lump
'Cause you dunked it in your cuppa.

I know it's petty and terribly so.
You could have done much worse, I know.
But I think I'll have to let you go,
'Cause you dunked a muffin in your cuppa.

It seems that all men I know are bums.
The pain is intense and reality numbs.
When I washed up your cup it was full of soggy crumbs
From the muffin you dunked in your cuppa.

The standards I have are high, it's true.
I thought I'd spend my life with you,
But what you did just made me wanna spew.
You dunked a muffin in your cuppa.

A CREAM TEA STATE OF MIND

I'm rapping with my tray
And I'm gonna move your way.
This is what I have to say,
'Cause what I need today
Is a cup of Earl Grey.
That would be most pleasant.

You know what is new?
It's the things that I do.
I spit my rhymes so hard
And they're coming at you.
I hang out with my crew
And my homies too,
And I say, 'Hey, lads,
Would you care for a brew?
One lump or two?
I'll be mother, shall I?'

I'm a funky mother cuppa lover,
Got a cuppa with my supper
'Cause my plans you cannot scupper.
Put no milk in, watch me splutter.
I'm the bread and you're the butter.
I got a scone, too.
Add it to my song.
Gonna make it disappear.
'S gone.

Yo, 'sup!
Pass me your cup.
If you want to have a coffee
Then I guess you're out of luck.
I got a caddy.
Who's the daddy?
Who's the daddy
With his caddy?

I got a decaf,
Makes me dozy,
Got a teapot,
Got a cosy,
And I like milk in last
If you really must be nosy,

'Cause I'm wild and I'm free
And it's banging, you see,
'Cause seriously
This is all about tea.
This is all about tea.

HIGH TEA

My dad would lift the teapot up
And pour a thin trickle of tea
Into the cup far below,
And he'd say,
'Look, high tea!'
And we'd all roar with laughter.

Perfect equidistance,
Holding the strainer dexterously
So that it intercepted the
Warm tea stream,
Catching mini clods of tea leaf
In its dented wire mesh,
His perfect aim assuring
That the tea ended up
Just in the cup.
'High tea!' he'd say,
And we'd all roar with laughter.

So he'd experiment,
Stand on a chair,
On a footstool,
And then on a
Stepladder,
Anything to gain the
Necessary elevation,
And each time the tea
Ended up ever so neatly
In the cup
And we'd all roar with laughter.

One day, while he did this,
A passing ice cream van backfired,
Yet not a flinch did we see,
His aim as perfect as ever.
'Look,' he said, 'high tea!'
And we all roared with laughter.

The next day
He climbed a forty-foot ladder.
'High tea!' he yelled,
And we all roared with laughter.

And the day after that
He hired a hot air balloon
Piloted by a chap with an
Exuberant moustache,
And he climbed in the basket
And it took off
And went up and up
Until it was just a speck
In the sky
And, just as he was about to repeat
His usual joke with the teapot,
A sudden gust of wind
Blew the hot air balloon over the horizon
And we never saw him again.

'I didn't like that teapot anyway,'
Mum said,
And since then we've used teabags.

TODAY, I SHALL MOSTLY DRINK TEA

Today, I shall mostly drink tea.
And make the occasional wisecrack.
And I'll try to make people laugh.
And I'll dance on mathematics,
And I'll do other things, too.
But mostly, I shall drink tea.

Today, I will not lunge at anyone.
Today, I shall mostly not have a moustache,
And if the sun is too bright, I'll squint,
And I will not laugh at the unfortunate,
And I will just be myself,
Physically impossible as it is
To be someone else.
But mostly, I shall drink tea.

Today, I shall slither through people's consciousness
Like a computer virus,
And dance temptingly before the empty house of my darkest
    dreams,
And push up life as if it's a sash window,
Letting the love flow in as if it's fresh air,
And be retweeted by a ghost
And do the washing up,
But mostly, I shall drink tea.

Today, I will have eyelashes,
And I will breathe;
I'm doing it now.
And I will take my linen suit
Out of the tumble dryer
And tell it a joke
And watch as it creases up,
And I will act like a grown-up,
But mostly, I shall drink tea.

And I shall jimmy and jitterbug, sway to imaginary rhythms, find hidden subtext in rhymes, shake hands, make friends, hide behind false veneers, wear masks, gel my hair, shower, wash off layers, hide from the world, be ever so quiet, shout it from the tiles, push TV aerials and watch them quiver, jive, dance, breathe, smile, laugh, write my name in the sand, eat, sleep, drink, tell jokes, cultivate punchlines, doze, live viciously, live with vehemence and try not to grab it all while making it look like it's no effort, like I'm really not that determined, like these things just happen, today I shall live sublime and do all of the above with the absolute screaming conviction that this, oh, this, yes, this is life!

But enough about me.
Today,
Mostly,
I shall drink tea.

BURNSVILLE

The car is big, brash and American,
As American as a baseball game,
And, just like a baseball game,
It seems to go on forever.
The size of a frigate, this thing
Burns enough fuel to power a small city.
'You be navigator,' my uncle says,
Which is easy, as there's only one road
Here in the mountains of West Virginia;
Even I can't muck this up.
I catch my reflection in the rear-view mirror.
You're a long way from Basingstoke, sonny Jim.

We're on a road trip through America.
The scenery and grandeur are simply stunning,
But I haven't had a sausage roll in ages.
A teenage lad,
Overcompensating his obvious campiness
By wearing an Arsenal football shirt
(I have no idea who Arsenal are;
I just like the fact they've got
Arse in their name),
And my uncle looks like Leslie Neilsen.
No wonder that diner back there
Went very quiet the moment we walked in.

And jeez, I've become so terribly English.
The Americans really seem to like it.
A waitress made me read from the TV guide
And she couldn't stop laughing.
And no, I've never met Benny Hill.
Why is everyone here obsessed with Benny Hill?

A muggy, huggy, humid day.
The moment I step from the car,
Everything goes moist.
The constant heat has led to some serious chafing.

As the sun sets, the highway announces
A small town called Burnsville.
We stop for the night.
Leslie Neilsen swings the frigate off the freeway
And we book into a small motel.

The adjacent highway sighs
As if it's all too much.
The hillsides loom,
The neon buzzes.
Passing trucks growl and
The world smells of diesel,
Melting tarmac and decomposing weasel.
It's gritty,
But not in a Harold Pinter sort of way,
But in the way that grit is gritty.
There's something sticky and
Unsettling in the heat of the night,
A bit like finding half of a frog
In a packet of crisps.
Restless dreams in wooden homes,
This covered fold, this
Hidden valley, and me,
Jolted up from hours of driving
And awash with hormones and teenage desires,
Suddenly turned on by absolutely everything,
Which I can only quell by singing
The refrain of a TV advert for Bran Flakes.
'They're tasty, tasty,
Very very tasty!
They're very tasty!'

My room is hot.
I've seen these places
In so many films.
A bed, a bathroom, a Bible.
I open the window and the moths fly in,
Thousands of the fluttering bastards,
Moths on the TV screen, moths

Circling the lights, moths on the window frame,
And even the bastard moths are turning me on.
I try to bat them with the Bible,
But the Bible turns me on.
I try to shoo them out the door,
But the door handle turns me on,
And the door frame,
And the door turns me on,
And I turn off the light and then
Turn it on,
But even turning it on turns me on,
And I realise that I have to get away,
Oh yes,
I have to get away.
I place my hands on my head and through
Gritted teeth I sing,
'They're tasty, tasty,
Very very tasty!
They're very tasty!'

It's warmer outside, and dark, so dark.
I walk down to a dried-up stream
Behind the motel,
Turn and look at the wooded valley slopes.
It's all so quiet and ethereal, but, bloody hell,
After a while it starts to turn me on.
I tell myself there must be monsters here,
Gun-toting wild men,
World-hating survivalists,
Angry war veterans, how masculine,
How beautifully masculine,
Sensuous and masculine,
How it turns me on!
I try to look for some natural splendour,
But all I can see is a Coca-Cola machine,
Humming and electric and brash
And vibrating ever so softly, like a lover,
Which turns me on.
So I walk, I walk up to the main road,

The highway, long grass crickets chirruping
Like the springs of a bed,
Oh God! Back to the motel,
The motel where so many slumbering naked people
Have tossed and turned.
Oh dearie me,
How dreadfully even this motel turns me on,
And just as I'm thinking I should really
Get a grip,
I see the open door to the motel laundry room.

Bright-lit fluorescent glaring in the sultry night,
And two shining hot shirtless lads operating
The machines, nonchalant, slyly sexual, the
Glistening sweat causing their lithe bodies to writhe
And contort with an ethereal glow.
They're tasty, they're tasty,
Oh my, they're very, very tasty,
They're very tasty indeed.
And all of a sudden the motel is just a motel,
The moths, the crickets, the Coca-Cola machine,
The doorway and the light switch,
They are what they are,
And I am what I am,
And the lads, oh momma!
We all know what they are.
I go back to my room.
Boy oh boy,
Do I go back to my room!

The next morning we load
Our luggage into the frigate
And Leslie Neilsen asks me
What I'd like for breakfast.
For some reason I have a
Sudden hankering for Bran Flakes.

THE CALL OF THE MILD

Being the manly and masculine sort,
No stranger to sport, to the thrill of adventure,
Like any man ought,
How could I have passed up
The utter and immense joy of fishing,
Another macho pastime to prove to the world
My overwhelming and definite straightness?

The trees were evergreen and I was seventeen,
And I don't think northern Ontario had ever seen
A gayer guy than I.
If I had been any camper
I'd have been a Winnebago.
Tight T-shirt and the shortest shorts
And the kind of walk
That had been described by the man in the bait shop
As looking like I had a roll of lino under my arm.
I may have appeared,
Amid all this wincing
And uncoordinated mincing,
And the man in the bait shop who
Kept on winking,
Somewhat effeminate.

My uncle and dad were adventurers,
Doyens of blokey pursuits who
Were not at all put off by bears, wolves,
Physical discomfort, the pungent lake,
The biggest mosquitoes I'd ever seen and
The fact that it was one hundred miles from the
Nearest shopping centre fashion outlet.

'Tell me,' my uncle said, as we
Clambered aboard our steel-bottomed boat,
'You ever win any medals at sport?'
Before my dad could change the subject
I explained, somewhat joyfully,

How at the village fête
I'd got a bronze for my embroidery,
And for some reason
My uncle didn't ask any further questions.

Amid the gurgle of our Evinrude,
We pressed on into the wild northern solitude,
Past ominous woods whose evergreen heart
Have claimed many a mad soul and torn apart
Dreams of life in wilderness sublime,
Winter's icy fingers and the march of time
Leading humanity to a state of perpetual forget.
My uncle said I couldn't play my Abba cassette.
Apparently it would scare the fishes.

In the shade of a coniferous bank we stop,
Kill the prop and set up shop,
Put hooks in our bait, and wait, and wait,
And my dad and my uncle can only nod
When I say that I like holding the shaft
Of a very sturdy rod.
And then, for the next two or three hours,
Absolutely nothing happens.

This is what it is to be a man,
Embrace the outdoors,
To use your hands,
Become a hunter-gatherer,
Pride of the tribe,
And go back to a cabin
And heavily imbibe,
Living as a winner
As if life were the lotto,
Fishing by day
And spending the night blotto.
Can there be a more natural and blokey quest?
Well, yes, there's the Eurovision Song Contest.

And then I feel a tug, my float goes under,
At the same time a rolling rumble of thunder.
'A fish!' I say. 'It's pulling the line!'
'Thank God,' my dad says; 'about bloody time!
You've got to reel it in, boy, that's the deal.'
'How do I reel?' I ask. He says, 'With the reel!
Wind it and pull it, don't give up the fight!
Show it who's boss, use all your might!'

I tell you it was a fighter, this accursed fish,
With a demonic spirit and a sordid death wish.
It teased as it fought and I thought I would faint,
Yet I was ever so brave and I made no complaint
As I thrashed and I yanked and struggled and tussled
(My perfectly coiffured hair was now ruffled),
Until at last, with a mighty great yank,
Did it yield to my power, nothing left in its tank.

I gazed eye to eye at this devilish beast
And knew that for years I would regularly feast
On the story of how I had conquered a foe
In this land of forest and wintery snow
Where a man is a man and cheeks are aglow,
With a tear in my eye as we at last let it go,
Knew I'd never see how it looked cooked on a plate.
Apparently it was in danger of being eaten by the bait.

Two men and a boy set out that day.
And, actually, two men and a boy came back.
In the evening cool in deckchairs outside
Our lakefront cabin surrounded by woods,
Eaten alive by mosquitoes,
My dad and uncle drank whisky and pondered
On the meaning of life,
While I was in my bedroom,
Dreaming of shirtless glistening lumberjacks.

DAWSON'S LAKE

It was the first day of summer.
A warm breeze breathed through the juniper bushes.
We went down to Dawson's Lake,
Me and Emmy Lou, Mary Lou, Betty Lou and Simon,
The hot sun glinting from the chrome grille of our
1957 fire-red Lincoln convertible,
Changed into our swimming clothes and fell under the spell
Of our youthful exuberance.

The water was cool and invigorating.
We frolicked in the shallows and then lay on the
Sand banks, drying in the sun.
Mary Lou said that she was worried about sharks,
And we laughed.
Betty Lou said she was worried about axe murderers,
And we laughed.
Emmy Lou said she was worried about the
Representation of giraffes in the media,
And I laughed,
And then I realised that nobody else was laughing.

'I think I've found two grains of sand the same,'
Said Simon.
He'd brought a microscope with him.
'They're around here somewhere,' he said,
Looking at the ground.

I liked Betty Lou,
And I was about to suggest a session
Of heavy petting,
But her nose was running,
So we
Chatted about nuclear annihilation instead.

Emmy Lou brushed her long hair in the hot sun.
She said that her uncle once met the poet Hart Crane
While ice fishing on this very lake.

I didn't understand why anyone would go ice fishing
When you can make ice at home
Perfectly well
In your freezer.

Mary Lou turned on the radio
Just in time for Del Shannon's 'Runaway'.
During the chorus I
Urinated behind a rhododendron.
Emmy Lou brushed her long hair in the hot sun.
Simon tried to alphabetise the shrubs.
I carved my initials in the rotting carcass
Of an armadillo.
Emmy Lou brushed her long hair in the hot sun.
Mary Lou and Simon arm-wrestled over the last ham sandwich.
Emmy Lou wrote I love James Dean
On the side of a goose.
I urinated behind a rhododendron.
The radio played Elvis Presley's 'Jailhouse Rock'.
Simon used the car door mirror to
Apply his lipstick,
Wrenched it clean off the car.
Betty Lou gouged a Pepsi and belched so loud
A flock of geese took off in fright.
Emmy Lou brushed her long hair in the hot sun.
The radio played Del Shannon's 'Runaway' again.
Mary Lou upchucked over the hot dogs.
Emmy Lou shrieked because she thought she saw
Richard Nixon in the undergrowth.
I urinated behind a rhododendron.
The radio played Buddy Holly singing 'Shaddap You Face'.
I urinated behind a rhododendron.
I think I might have a problem.
Emmy Lou brushed her long hair in the hot sun.
The radio played Del Shannon's 'Runaway'.
Our lives are small and meaningless.

LUST IN SPACE

He was the firm-jawed space captain,
Star of the sci-fi show.
Randy, tough, morally upright
And handy with his fists,
All manly macho sock-it-to-me-big-boy.
That all-in-one spacesuit
Leaves nothing to the imagination.
Oh, look, you've torn your shirt again.
The whole galaxy can see your left nipple.

Each week millions would tune in
To see him fighting rubber monsters
In crêpe paper caves
In a universe full of suspiciously human-like aliens,
And he was ever so handy with his laser beam,
Not one strand of Brylcreemed hair out of place
As he skipped over polystyrene boulders,
Followed by his bumbling old duffer of an assistant.
'You run off and catch up
With those cardboard robots.
I'll sit here for a bit
And get my breath back.'

His affable assistant
Told the producers he could take no more.
Fifty-eight years in Shakespeare; he'd played the Great Dane.
'Hamlet?' they asked. 'No, Marmaduke the dog.
A stirring performance nonetheless.
I'm getting too old for this,
Even that episode we did in the land of the
Incredibly Slow-Moving Slug Aliens.
Plus I'm getting typecast
As an old man.'
'You're seventy-eight,' they pointed out.

At the end of season six he was killed off,
Quacked to death by giant space ducks,

And that's how I ended up on the show.
I mean,
It was pretty camp already, right?

First day on set I suggested,
'What if, you know, as a joke,
I get a bit aroused by the captain's
Shirt getting ripped?
I mean, it happens every week.
It would put a different spin on it.'
'Sure,' they said.
And when we were held captive by the
Gargantuan lizard men of the planet Gargantua
Amid an array of special effects,
I said, 'Hello, boys!
All that growling!
You sound just like my ex!'

To the maniacal and scheming demon wizard,
While supposedly undercover,
I said, 'Oh, you're so butch!
You must get it from your mother!'
While running away on Forbius Seven,
Pursued by the furious Forbius Sevenese,
I adlibbed the line, 'Oooh! A pair of handcuffs!
Now, what shall we do with these?'
Wink wink.

To the giant and not-at-all made of bubble wrap
Mega octopus
Who wouldn't let us pass,
I yelled, 'Oooh, you've got a face
Like a slapped arse!'
And in season seven episode six, as the captain
Reached out to deactivate space spiders
With the determined flick of a switch,
I reduced the whole studio to peals of laughter
By shouting, 'Brace yourselves, bitch!'

And every time the captain took out his ray gun,
I'd say,

'Don't point that thing at me!'
Or
'Gosh, that's a big one!'
Or
'Does it shoot as well as it looks?'
Or
'My, my, you've polished that one up nicely!'
Or
'Look at the shaft on that!'
Or
'Big ones are so much harder to conceal!'
Or
'Is it difficult to get a good aim with one that size?'
Or
'I've never seen one that shape before,'
Or
'Keep it covered up, big boy; I've just had a sausage!'

It was at this point that things started to get a bit silly,
The script deliberately mentioning
Black holes, being probed,
Weird openings, ventilation shafts,
Portals, protuberances,
And my dialogue replete with such gems as
'Captain, it's so hard!'
'Gosh, I've gone all stiff!'
'I think I really should get a grip!'
'Captain! We're going down!'
And it was only when we visited
The planet of the Giant Quivering Throbbing Prodders
That I thought,
How are we getting away with this?

It wasn't to last.
That night I was photographed
In a restaurant with my boyfriend Steven.
And next morning I was fired.
'We had no idea,' they said.
'We had no idea…'

SCRATCH 'N' SNIFF HIEROGLYPHS

I swear the sand granules had actually managed
To reach my boxer shorts.
Something was irritating like a bastard down there.
No wonder the camels looked so mardy.
I don't know how you talked me in
To being at the opening of the tomb.
'Don't get the mummy's curse,' you said.
'Here, borrow my crowbar.
I'll stand way back.'
I said,
'Is this some kind of pyramid scheme?'

Your rakish moustache made a mockery
Of the afternoon,
And when I hid your helmet you said
I was taking the pith.
'Put your nose to the wall,' you said,
'And have a sniff.'
'What's that?' I asked. 'Cinnamon?
Summer fruits?'

Give me a whiff of your hieroglyphs,
Your hieroglyphs, your hieroglyphs,
Give me a whiff of your hieroglyphs,
I'm sure they smell quite niiiiiiice!
Om pe om pe om pe om pe.

This one here is strawberry,
Scratch 'n' sniff, scratch 'n' sniff.
This one here is caramel,
Scratch 'n' sniff, scratch 'n' sniff.
Your colleague from the University of Basingstoke
Got the mummy's curse from the
Pharaoh down the street.
Now his soufflés just won't rise.

Give me a whiff of your hieroglyphs,
Your hieroglyphs, your hieroglyphs,
Give me a whiff of your hieroglyphs,
I'm sure they smell quite niiiiiiice!
Om pe om pe om pe om pe.

We shimmied down the tunnel to the tomb,
Shimmy shimmy shimmy boom boom boom.
Your moustache was so wide we got wedged
And I said,
'Will this be like *Raiders of the Lost Ark*?'
And you said,
'Egg sandwiches, please.'
I don't think you heard me.

Give me a whiff of your hieroglyphs,
Your hieroglyphs, your hieroglyphs.

The further down we went, the more pleasant
The flavours,
Scratch 'n' sniff hieroglyphs.
'I can't wait to get a whiff
Of those in the sarcophagus,'
I ventured.
'Sonny Jim,' you replied, 'at the
Opening of King Shufflebum the Pungent,
I got my wristwatch caught in his bandages.
Accidentally
Spun him around like a spinning top!'

Give me a whiff of your hieroglyphs,
Your hieroglyphs, your hieroglyphs.

'Just six more corners to go,' you said,
And then we stopped to admire
The hieroglyphic badgers,
Venerated as they were by ancient Egyptians.
Badgers in their natural habitat:
A wholesale carpet warehouse,

The reception room of a chiropodist.
'What the fuck?' I said. 'What the actual fuck?'
A scratch and a sniff.
'Hmmm, avocado!'

Give me a whiff of your hieroglyphs,
Your hieroglyphs, your hieroglyphs.

'Here we are,' you said, 'at the entrance
To the tomb of the Pharaoh Steve.'
I wonder what the scratch 'n' sniff will be.
I wonder what the scratch 'n' sniff will be.
'Behold, a sensory overload!' you said,
Your moustache quivering,
Your voice warbling,
'And beware of the mummy's curse!
You might never operate a spork again!'
We went right in and, wouldn't you know it,
Some bastard had put up wallpaper.

Give me a whiff of your hieroglyphs,
Your hieroglyphs, your hieroglyphs,
Give me a whiff of your hieroglyphs,
I'm sure they smell quite niiiiiiice!
Om pe om pe om pe om pe.

HOME DELIVERY MAN

Home delivery man, home delivery van,
Cubicle of light in the night,
Rattle those crates, those great crates,
Cheese in the crates, cheese grater crates.
Don't bang your head on the door, love.

You're a high-vis whiz; you mean biz.
You know what's what and what's what is,
With that giant face of the man painted on your van,
The man on the van grinning at a stick of broccoli
On a fork.
Imagine being a model and your career's
Going down the pan, just about done,
No more yachts, just a phone call
From your agent: hello, here we go,
Can you grin at a stick of broccoli on a fork
And we'll put you on the home delivery vans?

Rattle those crates, you bastard god.
What have my neighbours ordered now?
Open the net curtains just a crack.
Is that couscous, or is that not couscous?
I've never had much of a sense of hummus.

Home delivery man, home delivery van.
This whole road is a cavalcade of wankers,
But your rippling biceps have made a mockery
Of the afternoon.
Did you see me looking out between the net curtains?
Came back from the toilet,
Jesus Christ, there's a freakishly big head
At the end of my garden path.
Oh, it's just the
Man grinning at the stick of broccoli painted on your van.

Home delivery man, home delivery van.
Is that a two-litre bottle of Vimto

Or are you just pleased to see me?
Would you like to pop inside for an impromptu
Karaoke session?
My mate Brian sang acapella with the door-to-door
Chiropodist.
I've got the mic set up and a Spandau Ballet backing track.
Come back,
Come back,
Home delivery man,
Come back.

YAY!

In a sunbeam fortuitous, each
Coffee shop tabletop crumb throwing a mini shadow,
Does he sit fervently cradling a cooling cappuccino,
Barely able to sip lest fortune dance past,
Eyes scanning the dwindling queue,
His heart beating, *yay*.

The sensuous moment he knows is prone to natural erosion,
That prime of life and passions abloom, and souls
Similarly fertile should match by chance,
Flowers opened before a miracle sun
Whose radiance burns with more than caffeine and
Dating app algorithms, *yay*.

His voice would surely choke a dry shriek,
For love has seldom been convenient or easy,
Too socially naïve to pluck up night club courage
Or contort his lithe frame to those convoluted motions
Required by laser beam rhythms, his only quick and nifty steps
Being those two ahead, *yay*.

The floor and the walls are superfluous,
The chatter of adjacent table natterers
Mattering less than this one moment in which
He might as well pick from the ether between
Thumb and forefinger the future itself,
Two paths, two destinies, *yay*.

It's a miracle only that so many millions before had
Previously been so lucky; that morning he'd
Looked in the mirror and felt that same luck
Of lasses through the generations, yet luck
Would soon be stripped by the years, and his luck
Would disappear, yay?

Lovers in a moonlit copse, lovers in a row boat,
Lovers in a church or a chapel in grinning disbelief,

Lovers in Renaissance art, lovers in a lonely hovel.
Every soul that ever had the chance has loved,
Or at least had the capacity to do so.
It's more than biology, *yay.*

Kneeling Lord Byron kissing the hand of a suitor,
Star-crossed sprites and Venus aflame,
Knights of the realm in chivalric honour,
Cherubs with bows, blushing hearts,
Venus in heat and roses aglow,
And him? *Yay!*

He looks up from his lucky table, sees
A familiar face at the back of the queue.
Their eyes meet once, a smile of
Internet anticipation, and then a nervous grin,
Words forced out past pumping chest:
'Hi, how are you?' *Yay!*

DRY-STONE WALLING

'Why have you never been dry-stone walling before?' he asked.
It was cold and wet and windy and foggy and miserable
And the rain was clingy and uncomfortable as it rolled down
    my neck.
'I have no idea,' I replied.

'There are two steps to dry-stone walling,' he said.
'Picking up the stone and putting it in the wall.
It's that simple. Even an idiot can do it.'
I gave it a go and a mini avalanche ensued.
'You're doing it all wrong,' he pointed out.

'Grab the stone like this,' he said. 'This is a little life hack for
    you,'
And I thought, *My life hack would be*
'Don't go dry-stone walling', but I smiled and I imagined
That each rock was a cupcake and I was making a
Display of cupcakes in a shop that sold cupcakes, but then
All I could think about was wanting to eat a cupcake.

'Do you like my beard?' he asked. 'I got it caught
In the zip of my anorak last week, and the missus
Had to cut me out with her giant dressmaking scissors.
By the way, what's this sudden trend I see for men
Wearing ankle bracelets?' I told him I didn't know.

'It's good to get out in the world,' he said.
'It's good to commune with nature, it's good to get
Your hands dirty, it's good to smell the pungent aroma
Of defecating cows, it's good to shiver.
It's good to have your fingers so cold they've gone numb
And bright pink, isn't it?

'You can always come back to my croft when all this is done
And take your shirt off, and your jeans look wet, too.
See how I use a piece of string to make sure we're
Dry-stone walling in the right direction? My wife says

She's out for the rest of the afternoon.

'It's good to be at one with the land, it's good to
Work with natural objects, it's good to feel the same
Ancient wind that blew on our ancestors, I'm getting
A trampoline delivered tomorrow if you ever want to come
Round and trampoline surrounded by rugged horny sheep.'

The dry stones I'd put on the wall all suddenly came
Tumbling down and we both stood there and he said, 'Yes,
I know exactly what you did there, got too greedy, my son.
You came in all cocky, thinking you're Jack the Lad
Of the dry-stone walling community, but it bites you on the arse.

'It's good when your nose runs and there's no choice but to let
    it drip.'
There's a small local bus I see every now and then whose route
    number
Dances like a digital will-o'-the-wisp above the dry-stone walls.
    I could have been off
And away before Neighbours came on, but that trampoline
    sounded quite tempting.

POET IN RESIDENCE ON A FISH FACTORY SHIP

I'm feeling a bit queasy,
This old rusty ship flung round like
That Danish weather girl in the
Last series of *Strictly*.
Last night I was sick in my
Left wellington boot
And only remembered this morning
When I put it on.

Sam is our captain.
He's seen it all, has Sam.
Freak waves, ghost ships,
An albatross
With a beard.
He's the finest seaman I've come across!
And James is our cook.
He can whip up the fluffiest meringues this side
Of Portland Bill.
And Jim, and Keith, and Stinky Pete.
Merry mariners, saucy seafarers,
Not one of them interested in bloody poetry!

I was so cold last night
That my nipples went really big.
I had a weird dream
That I was stroking a caterpillar.
And in the morning Keith said,
'Gosh, my moustache feels really smooth.'

Oh, the banter!
This morning I was laughingly called
A barnacle-encrusted puke-soaked
Impertinent half-witted buttock,
And I said,
'Nice to hear from you too, Mum.'

Out on deck,
Hauling in a big load with Jim.
'Do ships often sink?' I yelled,
Above the clatter of the engine.
He replied, 'Usually only the once.'

Gutting fish with Bill.
Been at it his whole life, has Bill.
Looks one way, then the other,
And says,
'Sonny Jim,
Have you ever been sexually aroused
By a walrus?'
I replied that I hadn't.

And a giant octopus stole my cheese sandwich,
And a sperm whale
Tried to mate with us,
And I was winked at
By a squid,
And I'd never seen so many crabs!
And our captain was out on deck
With a jumping rope,
Jumping up and down.
I suppose that's why they call him
The skipper.

And the sea got rough
As the ship rose up
Through swell and wave
And the skies spat rain.
They were ever so brave,
This lonely tub
On the wide wide sea.
Perhaps this was the wrong moment
To tell Stinky Pete
That he would make my life complete.

He slapped me
With a gurnard.

THE LIGHTHOUSE

Until the day I snuff it
I will always regret not being
A lighthouse keeper
Bearded or otherwise

My rock-hard
Pert-bricked
Tower
Visible from the cliffs
People pointing
Perky beacon-like
Pert-bricked
Tower
Long and spindly, it just
Kind of sits there
Atop
Rocks
Sturdy
ROCK-hard
Spewing forth
Solid beams

Whoosh, go the beams
See it rising from the spume
I hope I save some seamen tonight
Many a sailor has
Personally thanked me
When the waves are crashing
Having been saved
From oblivion
By the sight of me flashing
I
Blow
My
Own
Foghorn

Sailors pop round
My lonely beacon
And fly the Jolly Roger

My rock-hard
Concrete base
Proud erect
Ribbed shaft
Architectural
Slender yet strong
Protuberance
Imagine it
Perpendicular!

Made out with Andy
Right next to the lens
And the revolving mirrors
Came on as we affected the most
Primal display
Unwittingly beamed live on the
White cliffs of Dover
Well, there's
Another one ticked off my bucket list

Pert-bricked
Precarious on a reef
So treacherous
It could sink a frigate

'Would you like me to take
You up my spiral staircase?
Up and up and up and up
Some get dizzy and
Most get sick
And when you get
To the top
Ooooooh, it's a long way down
Ooooooh, I can't bear to look!'
I'll ask

'Do you like my cardigan?
Do you like my beard?
Do you like my lamb chop sideburns?
You're a long way
From the mainland
Mrs Henderson
Ooooooh, it's a long way down
Once there was a wave so big
An octopus
Got stuck on the glass
Slowly oozed down the window
It put me off
The thing I was doing'

Crazy colossal column
Creepy clammy corridors
Corroded catacombs
Cumbersome coastal
Computer-controlled
Clammy castle of
Consternation
Covered in crabs, this
Constant cursed companion
And its continuous castaway
Contemplating copulation
All day I've spent
Polishing the mirrors
Working to forget I'm alone
Working my fingers to the bone

My aunt was apt to remark
It looked somewhat like a sausage
And I suppose it does
Though I often liken it to a
Chunky Swiss roll
The kind you get in Asda
You need quite a head for heights
To operate at the
Very tip of it

Mmmmmmmmmmmmmmmm
You put on a long coat
And you walk into the
National Trust shop
Purchasing
A ceramic lighthouse

The man behind the counter
Gives you a knowing wink

SUNRISE

You become used to the toil, the noise,
The discomfort, the salt-flecked waves,
The aching limbs, the treacherous decks, the
Long hours, the constant motion, the
Tight space, and that sense of being at one
With a metal craft whose upkeep ensures
Your very survival.

But the sunrise is different every day.

Heading east, into a myriad of colours, the
Night lightens with a halo, or maybe a red
Stain which bleeds ever upwards, or else
Resplendent yellow setting afire the water itself,
Or maybe through a swirling mist the sun
Will be a red circle rising with a mystical intent,
Perfectly round, or perhaps the day will just
Kind of start, and we'll be on the bridge,
And the skipper will say, 'Come and see this,
Come and have a look.'

A new day
Reaches out its youthful hand
And plucks sweet chance from the hours to come.
The clock reset.
The planet still turns.
It's like the galaxy is smiling.

I SEE THE FUTURE

I see the future.
Resplendent souls enmeshed in rhyme.
I see the future.
Fortune skipping on a drum beat madly.
I see the future.
The comfort of friendship when times are tough.
I see the future
And I'm buff.
Like, really buff.
If I were any more buff
I'd be a buffalo.
That's what I see.

I see the future.
Passion rules the heart in tongues of flame.
I see the future.
I'm a psychic acrobat on the skateboard of hope
And I've got a floppy fringe
And I do that backwards head toss
That people with floppy fringes do.

I see the future.
Nobody has a bath any more, or a shower,
To save water.
Yet they're all pristine clean.
I see the future.
They've got ants, now,
Ants with microchips and little sponges.
Thousands of them.
You sit there
And they come out from their box
And give you a damn good scrubbing.
Thousands of scrubbing ants.
It tickles.
Part of your daily routine.

I see the future.
Forty shades of beige, as beige as my jacket.
Everyone wants to be beige, now.
Beige.
I see the future.
Thousands of ants.
Beige ants.
They're made by Elon Musk.
They've all got little damp sponges.
I think I mentioned that.

I see the future.
Psychic shopping.
You think of something and you've bought it.
That's how I ended up with a lawnmower.
I don't have a lawn.

I see the future.
The ants are swarming all over me.
Hybrid ants, half-ant, half-android.
They're antdroids.
Microsoft tried the same thing
With slugs.
It was just disgusting.

I see the future
And I'm with you, my love,
My only, Cyborg Josh.
Where's the WD-40? You're
Squeaking again, dear.

I see the future.
All the ants are well trained; they just go
Back in their box once it's all done.
And they rinse out their little sponges,
And I feel fresher than a summer daisy.

I see the future.
Laughing and smiling in the oneness of being.

I see the future.
Happiness injected straight into your brain.
I see the future.
Justin Bieber says I'm too old to be riding a skateboard.
You see him in my backyard,
Dancing with the badgers.
Dance, Justin, dance.

I see the future.
The ants,
They've got these little sponges and each one
Concentrates on a different part of your anatomy.
Elbow specialists.
Arsecrack ants.
The number they send depends on your body mass.
Apparently I require 1,132.
It's something people brag about on social media.
'Look at me:
I'm down to a thousand!'
Ants.
Ants.

I see the…
The ants are just like regular ants.
They really get the grime out from under your fingernails.
Swill your mouth with them
And they'll work on your teeth,
Wearing microscopic breathing apparatus
And carrying little fluoride brushes.
Tiny little brushes.
Tiny little ant brushes.
Crawl upon my fearsome body, you
Insectoid cyborg products.
Charge them up with a USB socket.
Alexa, bath time!
Here come the ants!
Ants.
Even the pot plants are robots.
Ants.

I see…
Brings a whole new meaning to the expression
Ants in your pants.
My pants have never been fresher.
Ants.
Ants.
Fresher pants.
Ants.
Thresher ants.
Ants.

I see the…
That man who died,
They found his skeleton.
Ants.
They found his skeleton.
Ants.
Just happened to have his dental records with him.
Ants.
That's handy.
Too many cyborg cleaner ants.
Brings a whole new meaning.
Ants.
Brings a whole new meaning.
Ants.
Brings a whole new meaning
To deep cleaning.
Ants.
Ants.
Ants.

I see the futu…
I see
I see the fewwwwww
Ants
Ants
I heard them.
I heard the ants.

They were saying, *Tonight,*
We get him.
Ants.
Tonight we get the fat bastard.
Ants.
Ants.
Ants.
I see the future.
I see ants.
I see the future.
I see ants.

OSTRICH METAMORPHOSIS

Ostrich, your thin neck pokes up-beak,
Spindly-throat beaky-beak,
Between the other shuffling passengers
Ordering crisps at the buffet counter
On a train heading west.
(Clickety-clack, clickety-clack)
Next stop is Bath Spa.

Mrs Lavender, in the seat next to yours,
Kept chatting about the weather,
But the conversation kept coming back
To your being an ostrich.
She really couldn't get over it.
Sure, you've got a natty bow tie
And a straw hat at a rakish angle,
But there's no disguising you're an ostrich.
Mrs Lavender is very *fond*
Of the *Daily Mail.*
(Clickety-clack, clickety-clack)
You don't really need crisps at the buffet,
But it gets you away from her
As she nods in agreement with
The letters to the editor.

One more shuffle forwards.
A snide comment from behind:
'Chinless beak freak,'
From the dude in the hoodie.
He's no stranger to a slap-up supper,
But you don't point this out,
And now he's saying,
'Bloody flamingoes,
Coming over here and
Nicking our crisps.'
(Clickety-clack, clickety-clack)
(Clickety-clack, clickety-clack)
How did he know
You wanted crisps?

But what's this?
You note with consternation
As you pass through the station
That your limp wings
Are beginning to mutate
Into metal poles,
Straight, erect and slightly rusty,
And your plumage is becoming
Knocked and dented metal,
And in place of your elegant legs
A giant rubber wheel
As the train clarkerty-clacks,
Zips fast over points and tracks.
(Clickety-clack, clickety-clack)
(Clickety-clack, clickety-clack)

Magic in the moment,
A miasma in the morning,
Spellbound eerie memory sublime
And fortune dancing in a fleeting sunbeam.
The train rocks and everyone
Does a sideways step,
Like we all do from time to time,
Train or not.
A bewildering of the senses,
A bewitching of the mind,
Reality whips like a bastard.
Where there was once an ostrich,
Now there is a *wheelbarrow!*

Buffet-counter man puts a call-out
For the train manager;
He'll put you in the goods van.
Mr Too-Old-For-A-Hoodie-But-Wears-One-Anyway
Goes,
'Where's that bloody emu gone?
And who's left a wheelbarrow here?
And why is it wearing

A bow tie?'

'Next customer, please.'

(Clickety-clack, clickety-clack)
(Clickety-clack, clickety-clack)

NATHAN WENT FOR A WALK IN THE RAIN

Nathan went for a walk in the rain,
Felt the cold drops sting, thrown by the wind
Like thoughts flung at him.
Often he felt he could disappear
Given the chance,
Less than a ghost,
Scared by its own haunting.
Often life
Really was too daunting.

Hands thrust in pockets,
He would stand under the
Limbs of a tree
Whose skeletal branches
Silhouetted against an overcast
Battleship sky
Seemed to him
The jagged black lightning
Of negative storms,
Moments of joy nullified,
Time turned inside out.
Even this tree, one day,
Would fall and rot,
Not even a memory.

Custodians of masculinity leer in with
Jeering grins,
Jagged claws soured with the blood of souls
Too weak to join the cultural dance,
Maps marked not with routes
But the chaos of headstrong toxicity,
The violence of difference,
For straying would be a calamity
And only a fool would sheer from the path
And be rightly and soundly mocked.

Nathan went for a walk in the rain.

It's hard to explain the indefinable.
It's easier to be a man and stamp down emotion,
To be one of the lads and aspire to such,
Show no fear, stick up two fingers at pain,
Don't be weak, don't be spineless,
And don't talk about it, don't talk about it,
And if someone does then don't listen.
For God's sake, don't admit that you're lonely.
What kind of man does that?

Nathan went for a walk in the rain.
He watched the puddles circle with heavy drops
Falling like abandoned ideas or dragon tears.
No time to explain, just a walk.
No time to talk, never time to talk,
No time to listen if he needed to talk,
And what could he possibly explain?
Nathan went for a walk in the rain.

TO THE CAR FULL OF YOUTHS WHO SHOUTED 'POOF' AT ME

Of course it might have been a lucky guess,
Though I held high in the Scottish drizzle
A rainbow unicorn umbrella,
Which even I concede was a little camp.
Or maybe my pink feather boa was
Poking out from my Tesco bag for life.
Or maybe they were just nasty bastards.

It wasn't like I was gawping at a fit bloke,
Or wearing my *I Like Cock* T-shirt,
Or logging into Grindr and shouting,
'Where are you, FunkyLoveMuffin?
Coooooo-eeeeee!'
I was on the way to buy a steak and kidney pie,
And you can't get any straighter than that.

As the car sped away
I felt the loving embrace of the generations who couldn't.
But did anyway.
Souls whose crime was to love,
But loved fiercely and with passion.
This thought, and my *rainbow unicorn umbrella*,
Added some glitz to a drizzly Tuesday morning.

What was it that gave the game away?
Did I flounce, did I strut, did I sashay?
Did I mince?
Does it matter?
No glitter in the drizzle, no secret street sequins.
I've been out and proud
Since before you were born,
Gayer than the gayest gay that ever did gay,
Though I do occasionally wear an anorak.

Like phantoms they come, Alan Turing,
Oscar Wilde, Freddie Mercury, Frank O'Hara,

Marcel Proust, Noël Coward, Quentin Crisp,
Their ghosts swirling along the Edinburgh cobbles,
Bert and Ernie from *Sesame Street*
And the anonymous lovers of old
Proudly flying the flag before it even existed,
Beating down the fear and marching brave,
Stonewall freedom fighters, Harvey Milk, a fist raised
Triumphant in the oneness of a gay new world,
That those for whom biology had different ideas
Might walk unmolested in the conscience
Of public acceptance.

And I, oh,
I might rise before you!
You will cower and tremble.
I, mighty gay overlord,
Will crush thy Fiat Panda betwixt my
Powerful thighs,
For it is I, prince of rainbows,
Puncher of preconceptions,
The Pink Avenger,
Exacting my just and fearful revenge
In the name of blessed queerdom!

But then
I just sigh,
And I say to myself,
'Some people
Are just tossers.'

THE QUEER EXPRESS

A tinsel-littered terminus on the greyest grey of days.
A gleaming marble concourse and a smoke machine haze.
Excitement builds in tight T-shirts, dressing to impress.
A train's due in at platform six; it is the Queer Express.

The chuffing puffing mother-huffing pumping disco train,
This gently swaying, high-heel sashaying, otherwise quite tame
Lip sync boa, something-of-a-goer power ballad queens,
Leather-clad sexy dad, this transport of my dreams.

Everyone is welcome as it thunders down the track,
A destiny that's shining bright, the rhythm of the clickety-clack.
Clones and drones feel so at home, and big butch bears too.
Take a seat on the Queer Express, carriages LGBTQ.

Our history is one of Pride and those who dared to stand
And fight the law and rise above; let's shake them by the hand.
And now there is sweet freedom sung amid the pumping beat.
The rainbow flag flies proud for you; hop aboard and take
    your seat.

This sequinned rocket, this tinsel train, there is no quiet zone.
The ultimate community where no one feels alone.
I climbed aboard twenty years ago, never again felt like a
loner.
A sexy hunk in the opposite bunk is giving me a…
Reason to be here.

This all-embracing heart-racing diesel-engined chuffer,
This laser choo-choo homo loco never will hit the buffer.
It's thundering and building speed and passing through the
    night
For souls in need who feel indeed that now the time is right.

There'll be moaners, haters, zealous types and those who
    don't agree.
The train is there for everyone, and that's what makes us free.

The point of life is that we live up to our history,
 And if you can't be what they want, you might as well just be.

The Queer Express is said by some to be an urban myth.
Stand by the tracks on a foggy night and see its glow in the mist.
The train exists in every soul who's felt the world's askance.
Hop aboard the Queer Express and join this blissful dance!

Everyone, welcome aboard.

THE GHOSTS OF PRIMARK

Late-shift shop staff gibber and quake and shiver
By the phosphorescent mannequins,
A spectre there in menswear,
A phantom in the pants,
And again the rattle of chains
By the counter dealing in refunds and exchange:
It's the ghosts of Primark.

Oozing from the floor, the eerie outlines
Of texting millennials
OMGing as they shriek like banshees amid the sarongs.
Zombie topknot latte baristas aquiver,
Ectoplasm on the escalators:
It's the ghosts of Primark.

The haunting swish of formless hands
Unable to operate touchscreen tills.
Headless horsemen agitated in
The hat section.
Shoplifter poltergeists lobbing cheap tat merchandise
And Egyptian mummies in onesies.
The deranged howl
Of a soul tortured in the fiery pits of hell
Refused a refund on a
Pair of cream chinos,
For some reason sounding for all the world
Like Frankie Howerd.
Ooooooo.
Oooooooo!
It's the ghosts of Primark.

This no-alcohol zone, awash with spirits.
The dungeon plundered, picking locks and six-packs of socks.
The low moan of the ghostly husband,
An apparition of arm-folded desperation
Outside the changing rooms.
He's still waiting.

After all these years, he's still waiting.
It's the ghosts of Primark.

The spooky outline of a phantom mechanic diesel fitter
Looming in the lingerie,
Holding up knickers and shouting,
'Diesel fitter!'
The ladies' underwear all comes alive,
Shouts encouragement to the more timid ghosts:
'You can do it, come on, you can do it!'
Such a great selection of support bras.
It's the ghosts of Primark.

Ethereal jackets and haunted macs.
I ain't afraid of no coats.
The spirit of a long-dead retail manager
Being chased by a vicar.
Mind you, he needed the exorcise.
It's the ghosts of Primark.

This cacophonous cavern of cursed cut-price clobber,
Duck fake selfie lips Instagram post ghost,
Chalky pastel ghouls and smart casual demons.
A howl of agony,
A shriek of dismay,
The rhythmic unearthly sway
Of the scrunchie display.
The unhinged delirium of lost souls traipsing,
Blank eyes staring,
Thumbs hitting send in supernatural tweets,
Flash sale price tag afterlife hashtag
Clothes hanger doppelgänger.
These lonely souls, these poor trapped spooks,
These retail monsters in polyester suits
Who once would laugh so happy and free,
Ladies and gentlemen,
They're you and me.
We are the ghosts of Primark.

PUG-MAN

Pug-Man, Pug-Man,
Who the hell is Pug-Man?
Half pug, half man,
Can catch a crook like any pug can.

Half man, half pug.
Don't give him a hug.
Just take him to the scene of the crime
And he'll use his pug-like tenacity.
Works every time.
Who's Pug-Man?
Oh my God, it's me!

And my sidekick would be
Spaniel Boy,
With his long ears and dopey demeanour.
We'd take any villain
To the cleaner!
Hopefully not the vacuum cleaner.
We're scared of the vacuum cleaner.

Upchucked vomit on the museum floor.
Upchucked pug sick.
The villain can take no more.
He's down!
It wasn't planned.
Just happened. Pug vomit.
Bad prawns.
Caught the bastard, though.
Pug power!
'You've done it again,' says the mayor,
'And here's a fifty-pound fine
For the vomit.'

Oh no, Professor Crescendo,
His finger poised over the button
Of his doomsday device.

Spaniel Boy started humping his leg!
'You've done it, Spaniel Boy,'
I said.
'Oh, was that the bad guy?
I didn't realise.'
Pug power!

And the shepherd,
His sixty-eight sheep run loose.
I sprang into action.
'There you go,' I said,
'I've saved your seventy sheep.'
'That's two extra,' he said.
I replied, 'Well,
I rounded them up.'

I have two special powers.
My pug breath can down a crook
At forty metres!
And I can bore people to death
With my poetry!
(That's not a particularly pug-like attribute;
That just always happens.)

I never reveal my identity.
A friend got close.
'Are you sure you're not Pug-Man?'
He asked.
'What makes you think that?
My inherent bravery?
My rugged masculinity?
My never-say-die attitude?'
'No,' he replied:
'Your wrinkled face, those rolls of fat,
Those stumpy little legs,
Your squashed nose and constant dribble.'
I changed the subject.

A cold foggy night.
Coming back from a trampoline competition,
Cutting through the cemetery,
I was bitten by a radioactive pug,
Eyes aglow.
Ten minutes later
A robber came a cropper on my slobber
And Pug-Man was born!

P is for *Pug-Man, come and save us!*
U is for *You bastard, I was going to have that half-eaten bacon
bap.*
G is for *Gee, what's that stench?*
Hyphen.
M is for *Most people don't appreciate the emotions lurking
within and the constant psychological malaise. Why won't
someone come and save me from this existentialist nightmare?*
A is for *A pug? They sent a pug? I'm trapped underneath an
upturned petrol tanker and they sent a pug? What's wrong
with the fire brigade?*
N is for *Now if that's a superhero, I'd hate to see an average
one!*

Faster than a basset!
More powerful than a particularly miffed Yorkie.
Is it a bird?
Is it a plane?
Is it a badger?
No, it's a pug.
Bloody hell,
It's Pug-Man!

SIDEBURNS

Those words were barbs which drew blood with each prick.
The taunting devilish grinnery of secondary school bullies
Always looking for the easy target.
Suburban yokels from commuter town districts
Whose mirth was perked because, apparently,
I had abnormally big sideburns.

Blame it on Bowlcut Suzanne, my local hairdresser,
Where no matter what you asked for you came out
With a bowl cut and the longest sideburns known to man.
'Sidies sidies sidie sidie sidies,'
My classmates would taunt,
And they had a point.
I must have looked a complete wanker.

Last to be picked for the football team;
No respectable side could abide sidies
Sidling by.
Sliding tackle lad unsubtle sidie-free slider striker,
Sideburns on the sidelines.
Didn't want to play their stupid game anyway.

Mother would shout at the bathroom,
'What are you doing in there?'
In front of the mirror with a trimmer
And my hands all a-tremor
And a spirit level.

Level up one side.
Level up the other.
Level up one side.
Level up the other.
Oh no, there goes my left eyebrow.

In the midst of playground joshing, a poetry
Of sorts unmatched:
These pint-sized Byrons.

That I should be complimented on my
Hairy crab pincers, my two tentacled octopuses,
My bucket handles, my dining-room curtains,
My fuzzy baboons.
'Keep them coming, lads, keep them coming.'

Going up the stairs on the bus home,
Suddenly wedged as my sidies stick
With static to the plastic of the bus company décor.
Please, somebody, give me a shove.
'What's the hold-up?'
'It's sideburns lad again.
Someone fetch the angle grinder.'

Sideburns, sideburns,
Lurking in the undergrowth.
Someone fetch a blunderbuss.
Bam bam bam!
(Flap flap flap!)

They were so voluminous that often
They would entice the most mild-mannered man
To enquire as to their structural integrity,
And every now and then
The offer of a fondle.
Sideburn fetishists online asking me to lean in
To the camera and comb them,
'Go on, comb them,'
And you know what that is?
Internet grooming.

Both had the appearance of having been
Drawn on by a drunk Muppet.

One day I was apt to declare,
'Your words cannot harm me,
For within lurks a beast of peace,
A man within whose heart doth sing

And hope for a time when people look
Beyond
These sprouty sprouty temple protrusions,
Draw their own conclusions,
You villainous band of slobbering
Half-witted blabbering pigheaded donkey-arsed
Cretins.'
(And that's when the vicar
Halted the harvest festival.)

Bereft of hope, my sideburns
A passport to little more than
Crippling self-doubt,
I knocked on the door of Bowlcut Suzanne
And showed her a picture of the latest trendy
Spiky-haired mullet.
She told me to sit and said,
'One bowl cut coming right up.'

MY MOTHER IS BANKSY

All of those years I spent
Assuming that my mother was not Banksy
Were completely nullified
When I found the spray paints and stencils
In the potting shed.
'No, I'm not Banksy,'
My mother said,
And I hadn't even been thinking that she was.
But I only thought that she was
When she said,
'No, I'm not Banksy.'

It's the gritty urban depictions of life
In all its rich variety,
Which previous to this she had only ever
Had cause to depict
In her crochet and flower arranging,
Now ingrained as those artistic
Renderings
On brick walls. She's the
Voice of a generation, the
Conscience of a society,
Feeding minds and souls the same way
She feeds with sausage rolls
And crisps.

Tracing the development of Banksy pieces,
They're all on her bus route.
She has a stepladder for the tricky bits.
'Why didn't you tell me you were Banksy?'
I asked.
'I didn't think you'd be interested,' she replied.

'And where did you get the name from?'
'Oh, I was in the bank, see.
I came this close to being called
Post Officey.'

She had afternoon tea with Stormzy
The other day.
And he did the washing up, bless him.
And then she freestyled with some hip-hop
Grime lads,
Incorporating a cracking recipe for steak pies.
I'm well jealous.
She never brings out the good china
When I pop round.

'It's hard to be an iconic figure of mystique
And social conscience,'
She sighed,
'And keep up with my soaps.
But don't you go telling anyone, now;
I'll be ever so grumpy.
You can mention it in one of your poems, though.
They don't get the same kind of exposure.
No offence.'
'Thanks, Muv,' I replied.

She's off again to Bristol this morning,
An early train, her tartan shopping trolley
Full of spray cans, and it
Rattles on the cobbles, all those little
Bearings in the cans a symphony of hope.
It all started twenty years ago
When she wrote the word Bollocks
On the wall of the bus station for no reason.
'Don't get arrested,' I said.
'Coming round for a roast on Sunday?'
She asked.

Lily Allen phoned.
'Is your mum in?'
'She's popped out,' I replied.
'Say no more,' she said. 'Wink wink.'

IN THE MOTORBIKE MUSEUM

In the motorbike museum
A hangar filled with bikes,
A café and a little shop,
All under the one roof.
The air is thick with spilled oil smells
As the chrome on the bikes gleams and glares
And, in the corner, a customer loo,
Just the one door, and one cubicle.
Amid the bikes that are slowly rusting,
I suddenly realise how much I'm busting.

A lady comes out, she holds the door,
And I go inside and do my biz,
Take a whiz,
The water tank still filling,
And with relief I pull the chain,
Wash and dry my hands, but
What is this?
The tank is still filling.

I pull the chain again,
But the result is just the same.
I pull again and again
And start to blush,
But there is no flush,
As I imagine a sudden rush
Of full-bladdered men,
That I should come a cropper
In this corner crapper,
The sound of aborted flushing
Amid a motorbike cornucopia
And slow tank filling
Echoing around the museum.

I take a break, and then
I start to count to ten,
And then I try again,

But the tank, it is still filling,
And even though I'm willing
Some pressure to make it flush,
My hopes, they turn to mush
As I imagine a crush
Of angry busting blokes
Forming a queue at the loo.

I wait some more
And try to flush again,
And again and again.
I try to flush once more,
And pull and crank and pull,
But the toilet is terribly fickle,
The water pressure just a trickle,
And my dignity is ever so brittle.
The tank is still filling up!

Again I count to ten.
Maybe that's plenty.
Better try twenty!
Then flush and pump and flush and flush,
My hand a blur on the chain,
Ga-danga, ga-danga,
Ga-danga, ga-danga,
Ga-danga danga danga
Ga-danga danga danga
Ga-danga danga danga danga danga
Dagga dagga dagga danga
Dagga dagga dagga danga
Dagga dagga dagga Dagga dagga dagga
Dagga dagga dagga Dagga dagga dagga danga!
Echoing round the motorbike museum.
Dagga dagga dagga Dagga dagga dagga danga!
Until the owner shouts,
'Hey,
Has someone started up one of my bikes?'

There is no happy end

To this ghastly tale.
I feel quite queasy
And look slightly pale.
I start to pray,
And then I wail,
'Please, oh, please, oh, please.'
I'd fall to my knees,
But the floor looks like
It could give me a disease.

So I wait,
And I wait,
And I wait,
And then I count to ten,
And then I pull the chain
Once again.

Ga-danga.

I just leave.
A queue of leather-jacketed men
Are waiting to go in.
'Morning,' I say to the first,
And then I get the hell out of there!

TWENTY-SIX WAYS TO HAVE YOUR LOVER LEAVE YOU

A was okay.
But he said he wasn't gay.
Even when we did
The things that are gay.
Then one day
He just went away.

B said he
Was the man for me.
Then B
Ran off with C.

D said he
Was free.
Then D also
Ran off with C.
That made three!

E came round
For afternoon tea.
But he dunked his rich tea
In his tea.
Goodbye, E.

F was called Jeff,
So I dumped him.

G whiz.

H was a fake
And a bit of a rake.
I think I made a mistake.
For goodness' sake.

I was a knobhead.
I was a complete bastard.

I was a bit of a wanker.

J would only stay
For a day.
'Stay, J,' I did say
At the end of the day.
He went away.

K said, 'Hey.'
I said, 'Hey, K.'
But, to my dismay,
He'd been out with J,
And J had stayed
For more than a day.
I didn't know
What to say!

L put me through hell.
I fell under his spell,
Though he had a strange smell,
On the stench of which
I don't think I'll dwell,
Like Camembert
Mixed with sweet caramel
And other things as well.
'Bloody 'ell, L.'

M was just like
The other men.
'I know you'll leave me;
Just tell me when.'
The clock struck ten.
He said, 'Right-o, then.'

N came then.
He said,
'Let's be friends.
Where does it end?'
I said,

'Just let me watch
The News at Ten.'
'Again?' said N.

O took it slow.
I told him to go.
'I've got things to do,
Don't you know, O?
Oh.'

P looked like a walrus.

Q joined the queue
Of those who would do
Nothing I asked them to.

R picked me up in a bar.
He didn't live far.
He said, 'Shall we do it?'
I said, 'Ha ha.'
He crashed his car.
Such a faux pas.

S was a mess.
I have to confess
I could love him no less,
But he'd never undress.
Sex with him
Was not a success.
I had to guess.
What a mess, S.

T stayed for tea,
Just he and me,
Though he ran out the moment
I went for a pee.

U, oh, U,
You bastard.

V said he
Would marry me,
Though he wouldn't carry me
Over the threshold.

W was trouble too.
I said, 'I want to cuddle you;
I hope it doesn't bother you,
W.'
He said, 'It does; goodbye.'

X is now my ex.

Y? You'd better ask X.

Z is now in bed.
I said to Z,
'You're the man for me.
Until I'm dead,
I think I'll love
You instead.'

I haven't found a reason
To break up with him yet.
In any case, I've run out
Of alphabet.

1234

Disco club
Underground
Booming bass
Pumping sound
Take my chance
Time and fate
I can't dance
It's too late
1234

Pulsing lights
Thumping beat
Old-school tunes
Stamping feet
I can't dance
On my own
I can't dance
All alone
I need drinks
Clear my mind
Turn back clocks
Turn back time
Alcopops
Single shots
Jägerbombs
Martini
Or perhaps
Cup of tea
1234

Trendy crowd
Trendy things
Skintight tops
Skinny jeans
Energetic
Flailing limbs
So surprised they

Let me in!
Try to show
My best move
Signal that I'm
In the groove
Something cracks
In my back
People think it's
A heart attack
1234

I want to dance
There's no chance
Someone's called
An ambulance
1234

DJ plays
Banging tunes
Modern stuff
Electropop
Eight hundred
BPM
EDM
I go up
Round the back
Ask him for some
Fleetwood Mac
He says no
1234

I need love
It can't wait
Ask a bloke
For a date
Or perhaps
Hours of sex
Oh my God
It's my ex

Sideways step
Sideways step
Sideways step
1234

See that man
Over there
Dancing in the
Laser glare
High cheekbones
Solemn air
Vacant stare
Perfect hair
Looks a bit like
Fozzie Bear
I go over
'Hello there
We would make
A lovely pair'
Says to me
'Don't you dare!'
Sideways step
Sideways step
Sideways step
1234

Feels right now
I'm on the brink
Think I will
Have a drink
Maybe that will
Help me think
Feel my hopes
Start to sink
Hang on, did
That man just wink?
I go over
To say, 'Hi
You are my
Kind of guy'

Says there's something
In his eye
Sideways step
Sideways step
Sideways step
1234

Not my night
Damn and blast
All my hopes
Never last
In the bin
Dreams are cast
Must admit
I'm aghast
I'm a relic
From the past
I am just
About to go
When a lad
Runs over so
Says to me
'Please don't go'
1234

Smile at him
I feel brill
Glad I waited
Here until
He went in
For the kill
Says to me
'I work the till
And you haven't
Paid your bill'
Sideways step
Sideways step
Sideways step
RUN!

SHAKKA LAKKA BOOM!

Shakka lakka boom boom,
Shakka lakka boom.

Gotta get through the day,
Gotta do your thing.
Gotta get through the day,
Feel it deep within.
Gotta get through the day.
People, make some room.
Can't do a thing without
Shakka lakka boom!

Go to bake a cake one day.
Go to bake a cake.
Go to bake a bake one day,
Hope I don't make a mistake.
Add all the ingredients,
Stir them with a spoon,
A little salt and a pinch
Of shakka lakka boom!

Shakka lakka boom boom,
Shakka lakka boom.

Made my Broadway debut
In a Shakespeare play.
I know all my lines by heart.
I know, just want to say.
'To be or not to be,' I said,
And, with a sense of doom,
Forgot what came just after that,
Said, 'Shakka lakka boom!'

Shakka lakka boom boom,
Shakka lakka boom.

Go out on a hot date,
Small talk and a chat.
Go out on a hot date
And then back to his flat.
Making lots of small talk.
Hope I don't peak too soon.
All he did was stroke my arm
And shakka lakka boom!

Shakka lakka boom boom,
Shakka lakka boom.

And then I went to the funeral.
My aunt had passed away.
Such a lovely funeral
On such a dismal day.
I went to give the eulogy.
The coffin lid went zoom!
My aunt, she suddenly sat right up,
Said, 'Shakka lakka boom!'

Shakka lakka boom boom,
Shakka lakka boom.

HAPPY

I can hardly describe it.
Often I get these moments
In which I'm able to stand back and
Look at my life as if from
A different vantage point,
And consider my journey
As a unified whole.
Boom, there it is,
I'm happy.
It's almost sickening.

Take my friend Mark.
They say, well,
He's only happy when he's got something to moan about.
Well, he is!
You should see him!
You should see his little face!
Having a good old moan
Really makes his day.
And that also makes me happy.

And then there's my friend Shane.
He's always happy.
He looks like a grin
With a person attached.
I say to him, 'You alright?'
And he says, 'Yeah, I'm alright.
You alright?'
And I'll say 'Yeah, I'm alright,'
And he'll say,
'I'm alright if you're alright,'
And I'll say, 'Alright,'
Because neither of us are big conversationalists,
But he's alright, is Shane,
And he's happy.

My favourite anecdote:
A glum theatre stage.
A set designer stands there
Having just decorated the scene,
Stands there with that gloom merchant,
Crinkle-faced Mr Intensity Samuel Beckett,
Turns to this existentialist deep thinker and asks,
'Happy?'

It's a fluffy puffy feeling.
It's incredibly appealing.
It's like a lack of gravity
That puts you on the ceiling.
It's a bouncy flouncy skip and hop
That makes your heart just flip and pop,
Smooth as silk and warm like tea
And sweeter than a lollipop.
Oh my,
Listen to me!

I'm not the sort to rise right up
And suddenly clap my hands.
I hope you understand.
'Cause this feeling
Is more a state of being
Than the status of this man.
Before you here I stand,
A soul enmeshed in mirth,
And it's been a constant feeling
From the moment of my birth
That every day
When I wake I say
Yay.

SEASIDE SURRENDER

I found an old photo
From the hottest day of the summer
Twenty years ago.
I'd just been for a swim in the sea,
And you'd taken it.
I'm on the green, dripping wet, in a
Strangely out-of-place Leeds United
Football top
And swim shorts,
Granules of sand stuck to my feet.

I remember
How cold the water had been.
I'd thought I wasn't brave enough
To go under once it started
Lapping around my nether regions.
I'd stood for a bit and just watched,
Jealous of the other swimmers,
Until, with dramatic effect,
I pinched my nose and plunged
Deep into the brine.

I'd gasped and spluttered.
But after a while it didn't seem so bad,
And I rather enjoyed it.
Though seaweed brushed my legs, I was
Worried that it was jellyfish.

In the plop of the water, I was visited
By sudden visions of beards and badgers,
The Titanic, cups of tea, camp cats, neon yaks,
A little house, surfer dudes, insomnia, a TV ident,
A New York cabaret stage, pink feather boas
And a friend who is probably straight.
They flashed before my eyes,
The opposite of drowning.
I'd never felt so alive!

On the green again,
Parched grass crunching underfoot,
I felt no different as I dripped,
Held my shoes and started walking back
With you to my nearby gothic bedsit.
You'd been waiting patiently the whole time.

ACKNOWLEDGEMENTS

First and foremost I'd like to thank my two best friends in the world of performance poetry, Melanie Branton and Samantha Boarer. Also Jamie Harry Scrutton, Tim Vosper, Becky Nuttall, Robert Sean Casey, Ziggy Abd el Malak, Jason Disley, Shelley Szender, Steve O and everyone else involved in the Torbay spoken word scene with its wonderful micro-climate of humour and whimsy. As ever, thanks to the Blue Walnut Cafe and the Artizan Gallery for your continued support, and thanks to Ian Beech for letting me use the photo on the cover.

Mark Tunkin, Anne Hammett, Steven Aske, Damian Rao, John Tomkins and my sister Angela Hammond, who are all on the outside looking in wondering what the flip I'm up to!

MargOH Channing, Dandy Darkly, Mark Wallis, Brandon Johnston, Penny Arcade, Flotilla deBarge, and all my New York friends.

Fellow Croydon Tourist Office band-members Bryce Dumont, John Samuel, Max Coulson.

To all those Robheads everywhere who come up to me and quote my own poems. 'Hey Professor of Whimsy! There's a badger in the garden who thinks he's on EastEnders!'

Thanks to my clowning director Dr Maggie Irving, who helps me find the funny and be braver, more physical, more downright silly!

Thanks to all those bookers, event organisers, festival curators, fringe companies, poetry and comedy show-runners who have booked me over the years.

And it goes without saying, thanks to Bridget, Clive and Harriet at Burning Eye.

I'm insignificant, I'm ever so small / In the scheme of things, I hardly matter at all / The latest thought, that I have thunk: / If I were a boat, I've probably sunk / But this is my book, and you've been reading me / Inside I'm jumping up and down with glee / Wheeee!

Lightning Source UK Ltd.
Milton Keynes UK
UKHW011851230421
382518UK00002B/110